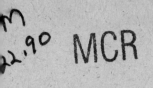

LOOK
CLOSER

An Introduction to Bug-Watching

Written and illustrated by
Gay W. Holland

The Millbrook Press
Brookfield, Connecticut

To my sisters, Elaine, Mary, and Ginny

Special thanks to Cheryl Ann Mack
for being the perfect bug-watcher

Library of Congress Cataloging-in-Publication Data

Holland, Gay W.
Look closer : an introduction to bug-watching / written and illustrated by Gay W. Holland.
p. cm. — (Look closer)
Summary: Describes a variety of insects and how they can be observed in a garden, in
open fields, in the woods, in water, and elsewhere.
ISBN 0-7613-2664-2 (lib. bdg.)
1. Insects—Juvenile literature. 2. Arthropoda—Juvenile literature.
[1. Insects.] I. Series.
QL467.2 .H64 2002 595.7—dc21
2001044465

Published by The Millbrook Press, Inc.
2 Old New Milford Road
Brookfield, Connecticut 06804
www.millbrookpress.com

Do you ever wonder what is really going on in a peaceful garden? There is no wind, yet the flowers shiver and dance. Why are they moving? What weird creatures lurk in the shadows? To see this strange bug world, you must look closer.

Bugs love flowers. These aphids suck up plant juice through the rostrum, a long hollow mouthpart, the same way you drink a milkshake through a straw. *Sluurp!* As they suck the juice, the aphids release a sweet fluid called honeydew. Ants like to eat the honeydew, so they protect and care for the aphids, like shepherds tending a flock of sheep. When you see lots of ants, look closer to see if they are herding a flock of aphids.

In the bushes growing in your yard, you might find a stink bug. The harlequin bug, a stink bug, produces a foul-smelling fluid. This fluid makes the harlequin bug taste bad to any animals that try to eat it. The harlequin bug's bright colors warn others that it is protected by a stinky smell.

While it sucks plant juice, the thornbug protects itself by looking like part of the plant it is eating. This disguise is so clever that you will have to look closely to see if it is a bug or a real thorn growing on the stem.

Open fields are full of bugs. What is that frothy white foam clinging to the tall grass? It is called "cuckoo spit," and it will not hurt you. Gently wipe away some of the bubbles and look closer. Under the foam lives the spittlebug, which is a young bug called a nymph. As the spittlebug sucks plant juice, it blows a safe "house" of bubbles and hides inside. When it grows up, the spittlebug leaves its bubble home and hops from leaf to leaf. So it is called a froghopper.

Another great place to bug-watch is along a country road. Among those goldenrod flowers an ambush bug is lurking. The ambush bug waits quietly, hidden deep in the flower's center. When a fly or wasp comes close—*Zap!* The ambush bug strikes, grabbing the wasp with powerful front legs and plunging its rostrum into the wasp's back. Next it injects a poison that turns the victim's insides to mush. Then the ambush bug slowly sucks up its soupy dinner.

Another good place to look for bugs is in the woods. The assassin bug goes out hunting for its food. It runs around until it finds another bug to stab with its long, sharp rostrum. Then it sucks out the insides of its prey. Don't get too close. The assassin bug can give you a painful bite.

Meadows of wildflowers are great homes for bugs. In the meadow lives the green lacewing, a beautiful bug with long, delicate wings and golden eyes. Gardeners like the lacewing because it gobbles up aphids, mites, and other bugs that hurt plants. It has a huge appetite and devours aphids quickly. Sometimes the green lacewing is called the "aphid lion."

On lazy summer days, the dragonfly is very busy. It loves to eat mosquitoes and grabs them right out of the air as it skims above the water. The dragonfly flies both backward and forward. Moving each of its four wings separately, it can hover in the air like a helicopter.

Under water, the water scorpion breathes air through a long tube that looks like a skinny tail. It lies in wait, hidden in the plants, until an unlucky tadpole happens to swim by. If you wade in the water, the water scorpion might think your big toe is just the right size to bite.

Your pets probably have a bug or two living on them down in their fur. If you see your cat scratching itself, look between the hairs. Fleas suck the blood of animals. Fleas have wonderful strong hind legs for jumping great distances. A cat flea can jump more than 200 times its height, 13 inches (33 centimeters) off the ground. If a 6-foot (1.8-meter) man could do that, he could skip taking the elevator and jump to the top floor of the Empire State Building.

The vegetable garden is a wonderful place for a close look. Some bugs love to eat the same delicious vegetables we do. Colorado potato beetles gobble up potato and tomato plants. They crunch and munch their way through the leaves and flowers. After they finish feeding, only the stems are left standing. Colorado potato beetles are greedy, fast eaters.

If you find an open sandy area on a trail, look closely at the ground. You may see a tiger beetle dashing along. The tiger beetle is a ferocious hunter. Like a tiger, it has large, powerful jaws and amazing speed. With its long legs, the tiger beetle is one of the fastest insect runners. Ants, which are swift runners too, are its favorite food. Don't try to catch it. Tiger beetles bite.

On warm nights when the sun goes down, a loud humming fills the trees. Did you ever look for the source of that noise? Look closer at the trees. Male cicadas sing their mating song every night. When young, as a nymph, the cicada lives underground, feeding on tree roots. It has a hard shell and big claws to crawl through the dirt. Then one night, the cicada climbs up out of the ground, splits open its shell, and emerges as a beautiful adult bug.

Right after dark, you can see tiny, blinking lights dancing in the air. Those lights come from the end of the firefly's abdomen. Some females, called glowworms, have no wings so they stay in the grass. The male flashes his special light signal on and off, and the female flashes back. This is how they find each other for mating. Sometimes a female will flash a fake signal to a male of another species to lure him close so she can eat him up.

The world of bugs is full of surprises.
Do you ever wonder what you will see if
you look even closer?

A World of Bugs

The world is full of bugs. For each human being on Earth there are over 200 million bugs. You can find them everywhere, from the hottest deserts to the coldest mountaintops. They have lived here much longer than we have. Insects, or bugs as we commonly call them, go about their daily lives eating, resting, and trying not to be eaten. We rarely see this "bug life" because it is so small. Through a magnifying glass, we can watch the secret world of these small gems of nature.

Insects play a vital part in our survival. Birds and many other animals depend on insects for food. We need them to pollinate our crops and flowers. Insects are also nature's perfect recyclers. Without them, we would all be wading around in decaying plants and animals. So the next time you say, "That nasty old bug," remember that life on this planet can get along just fine without humans, but life, as we know it, cannot exist without bugs.

Identification Guide

	3/8 in (1 cm)	Ambush bugs are spiny and jagged-shaped with big, strong front legs. They often catch prey much larger than themselves.
	1/16 in (0.2 cm)	Aphids have pear-shaped bodies and small heads. Some have wings. Their colors range from green to peach to pink to black.
	3/4 in (1.9 cm)	Assassin bugs are usually brown or black, and some have bright markings. All have small, long heads and sharp beaks for stabbing prey.
	1 1/4 in (3.2 cm)	Cicadas have broad bodies and shiny wings. If you look around the bottom of tree trunks, you can sometimes find empty brown cicada shells.
	3/8 in (1 cm)	Colorado potato beetles can be found almost everywhere in North America and Europe. They are easy to see with their yellow-orange and black stripes.
	2 1/4 in (5.7 cm)	Dragonflies have long, skinny bodies. They fly very fast, and many are brightly colored. Their huge eyes always touch on top of their heads.
	1/2 in (1.3 cm)	Fireflies are dark-colored beetles. They are easy to catch. If you cup one in your hands, you can watch its blinking light up close.

	1/16 in (0.2 cm)	Fleas have brown, hard, spiny bodies. Cat fleas are slightly different from dog or human fleas, but no flea is very particular about whom it bites.
	3/8 in (1 cm)	Harlequin bugs are stink bugs. Other common stink bugs are plain green or brown. Look on the undersides of leaves for masses of tiny barrel-shaped eggs.
	1/2 in (1.3 cm)	Lacewings all have long, clear wings with many veins. Besides the green lacewing, there are brown, black, and giant lacewings.
	3/8 in (1 cm)	Spittlebugs are very pale to match their frothy bubbles. They are nymphs, which means they are young bugs.
	3/8 in (1 cm)	Thornbugs belong to a family called treehoppers. Most treehoppers have fantastic shapes to fool their enemies.
	1/2 in (1.3 cm)	Tiger beetles have many different colors and patterns. They all have long legs, a long body, big eyes, and a bold attitude.
	1 in (2.5 cm)	Water scorpions are brown or black with scissors-like front legs for catching prey. They are found in slow-moving or still water.

Note:

Most of us call all insects "bugs." Entomologists (scientists who study insects) usually give the name "bug" or "true bug" only to insects in one order, Hemiptera. The insects in this book that belong to the Hemiptera are ambush bugs, assassin bugs, harlequin bugs, water scorpions, cicadas, aphids, thornbugs, and spittlebugs.

For more information on insects, try these sources:

BOOKS:

O'Toole, Christopher (Ed.). *The Encyclopedia of Insects*. New York: Facts on File, 1993.

Peterson, Roger Tory. *The First Guide to Insects*. New York: Houghton Mifflin, 1998.

Zim, Herbert Spencer, et al. *Insects: A Guide to Familiar American Insects* (Golden Guide). New York: St. Martin's Press, 2001.

INTERNET SITES:

http://www.earthlife.net/insects/six.html
http://www.insects.org
http://www.thebugpage.com